I0844194

UNSPOKEN HEARTS

journey of Hearts: Love, Loss, and Redemption"

By

JUNAID SHAHID

Table of Contents

CHAPTER 1

A FATEFUL ENCOUNTER

In the enchanting town of Willow brook, where emerald forests whispered secrets to rolling hills, lived a boy named Henry. His life, though seemingly ordinary, was about to take a remarkable turn. Each day was a slow, serene melody, with the occasional crescendo of youthful adventures alongside his younger sister, Emily.

But one morning, the tranquility of Willow brook was pierced by the arrival of Marya, a bewitching newcomer. She had transferred from an esteemed school in a bustling city, her family yearning for the simplicity of a small town. Marya was no ordinary girl. With hair as dark as the night sky and eyes that held the mysteries of the universe, she was a magnetic force that drew all eyes toward her.

CHAPTER 2

THE FIRST GLIMPSE OF ATTRACTION

Henry's first glimpse of Marya was during a radiant morning assembly. As she stood on the stage, her presence cast a spell on everyone who beheld her. Her smile was like the first ray of sunlight after a stormy night. Henry, usually the quiet observer, couldn't tear his eyes away.

Weeks passed, and he found himself irresistibly drawn to Marya's brilliance. She effortlessly conquered each subject, but her humility remained untouched. Her classmates admired her, but none as fervently as Henry. From his corner in the classroom, he watched her with a longing that grew with each passing day

THE JOKES THAT SPARKED A CONNECTION

One uneventful day, Henry summoned the courage to make Marya laugh. He had noticed her fondness for humor and believed that her laughter was the key to her heart. So, with a heart pounding like a battle drum, he dared to crack a clever joke during a dull math class. To his astonishment, Marya's laughter erupted like a beautiful symphony.

Henry couldn't believe his ears. Encouraged by her laughter, he embarked on a journey to become the class clown, sharing jokes that bordered on brilliance. Marya's laughter became the sweetest melody, and Henry reveled in the music of her joy. They shared moments of mirth and connection, but still, he couldn't bring himself to initiate deeper conversations. Fear of rejection gripped him tightly.

CHAPTER 4

THE UNWANTED STARE SAND CONSEQUENCES

As days turned into weeks, Henry's infatuation grew to an obsession. He watched Marya with unrelenting intensity, his gaze fixated on her as she moved gracefully through the school's corridors and attended classes. Unbeknownst to him, his stares became more pronounced, and Marya began to feel increasingly uncomfortable.

One day, Marya's discomfort reached its peak, and she made a bold move. She approached the stern school administration and lodged a formal complaint about Henry's behavior. The principal, known for her no-nonsense approach, summoned Henry for a severe reprimand. It was an experience that left Henry deeply humiliated and ridden with guilt

CHAPTER 5

A PAINFUL RETREAT

In a desperate attempt to avoid further consequences, Henry made the painful decision to cease his relentless staring. It was a decision that left him feeling as if he had lost a vital part of himself. He yearned for those stolen moments of connection that had been his only solace.

Despite his best efforts, their eyes occasionally met during class, and those fleeting moments of silent understanding filled Henry with a tormenting mixture of hope and despair. He yearned to engage Marya in meaningful conversation but was paralyzed by the fear of rejection.

CHAPTER 6

THE REJECTION AND GROWING DISTANCE

Desperate to bridge the chasm that had grown between them, Henry turned to social media. He sent a friend request to Marya, his heart pounding with anticipation. Yet, his hope was dashed when Marya promptly declined his request, casting him into a pit of desolation.

Undaunted, Henry messaged her, hoping to rekindle the spark of their previous connection. To his dismay, Marya's responses were icy and curt, each word a painful rejection. As time wore on, her replies became increasingly cruel, leaving Henry heartbroken and emotionally scarred.

The days turned into weeks, and Marya's irritation only intensified. In a heated exchange, she uttered venomous words, pushing Henry further away than ever before.

CHAPTER 7

A SECRET ADMIRER

Amidst the turmoil, there was one person who had been silently observing Henry's suffering—the ever-curious Emily, Henry's adoring younger sister. Emily admired her brother deeply, and watching him endure heartache tore at her young heart. Determined to help, she took on the role of Henry's secret messenger

CHAPTER 8

A
MISUNDERSTANDING

Emily became the clandestine bridge between Henry and Marya, passing notes and messages with the innocence of youth. Her efforts sometimes led to amusing misunderstandings, lightening the tension between the two. However, one fateful day, Emily misunderstood one of Henry's messages, turning a playful jest into a hurtful insult.

This misunderstanding triggered a heated argument between Henry and Marya, creating an even deeper chasm between them.

CHAPTER 9

THE UNSPOKEN LOVE

Two years passed, and life carried them in different directions. Marya's family once again uprooted their lives due to her father's job, and she bid farewell to the school. Henry never found the courage to express his true feelings, leaving him haunted by the specter of an unspoken love.

Henry pursued higher education, enrolling in a prestigious engineering university. Meanwhile, Marya followed her dream of becoming a doctor. Both of their lives took divergent paths, yet the memory of their unspoken connection lingered like a haunting melody.

CHAPTER 10

AN UNEXPECTED REUNION

Years flowed like a relentless river, and life moved on. Henry eventually found a loving partner who cherished him for his quirks and his imperfections. Marya, on the other hand, succumbed to the pressure of her family's expectations and married a wealthy man.

One radiant afternoon, in the bustling heart of Willow brook's grand mall, destiny wove its intricate threads once more. Henry and Marya's paths converged in a serendipitous encounter. Their eyes locked, and time seemed to stand still as they gazed at each other.

Unable to contain his emotions, Henry mustered the strength to approach Marya. His heart pounded like a thunderous drumroll as he poured out his feelings and bared his soul, confessing everything he had held back for years.

CHAPTER 11

A BITTER REJECTION

Marya listened in silence as Henry laid his heart bare. When he finally fell silent, she sighed and gently shook her head. "Henry," she began softly, "I appreciate your honesty, but I can't return those feelings. I hope you understand."

Henry's heart shattered into a million pieces, his soul crushed by the weight of her rejection. He nodded, trying to hide his tears. Though he had received closure, the pain was more profound than he had ever imagined.

CHAPTER 12

A TWIST OF FATE

As time flowed on, Marya's marriage became a dark labyrinth. Her wealthy husband was a distant figure, his attention consumed by business and social obligations. Loneliness was her constant companion, and the grandeur of her life a hollow facade.

Henry, in stark contrast, found solace and joy with his partner. Their love deepened with each passing day, a bond forged in the crucible of genuine affection and mutual respect.

Years later, destiny orchestrated another encounter between Henry and Marya. This time, Marya was burdened by the weight of her past decisions and the profound realization of what she had lost. She longed to apologize for her earlier actions, but the sands of time had slipped through her fingers

CHAPTER 13

LESSONS OF UNSPOKEN HEARTS

Unspoken Hearts" is a tale of unrequited love, missed opportunities, and the bittersweet lessons of life. It serves as a poignant reminder that love, though often marked by pain, can lead to self-discovery and inner strength. Henry and Marya's story reminds us that life's journey is filled with unexpected twists and turns, and sometimes, the most vital love is the one we find within ourselves.